CW00740723

Part of the England Coast Path

Text: *Dennis and Jan Kelsall*
Series editor: *Tony Bowerman*
Photographs: *Dennis and Jan Kelsall, Adobe Stock, Alamy, Dreamstime, Shutterstock*

Design: *Carl Rogers and Laura Hodgkinson*

Northern Eye Books

ISBN 978-1-908632-70-8

A CIP catalogue record for this book is available from the British Library.

Printed in the UK.

Important Advice: The routes described in this book are undertaken at the reader's own risk. Walkers should take into account their level of fitness, wear suitable footwear and clothing, and carry food and water. It is also advisable to take the relevant OS map with you in case you get lost and leave the area covered by our maps.

Whilst every care has been taken to ensure the accuracy of the route directions, the publishers cannot accept responsibility for errors or omissions, or for changes in the details given. Nor can the publisher and copyright owners accept responsibility for any consequences arising from the use of this book.

If you find any inaccuracies in either the text or maps, please write or email us at the address below. Thank you.

First published in 2019 by:

Northern Eye Books Limited
Northern Eye Books, Tattenhall, Cheshire CH3 9PX
tony@northerneyebooks.com
www.northerneyebooks.co.uk

 @northerneyebooks

 @northerneyeboo

For sales enquiries, please call 01928 723 744

Cover: *Ladram Bay, South Devon*

www.englandcoastpath.co.uk
www.northerneyebooks.co.uk

Contents

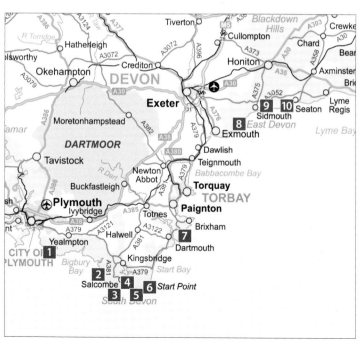

South West Coast Path

Running for 630 miles from Minehead in Somerset, around the tip of Land's End and back to South Haven Point at the mouth of Poole Harbour in Dorset, the South West Coast Path is Britain's longest National Trail. Bordered by the Bristol and English channels and looking out to the open Atlantic, it encompasses some of England's most spectacular and wildest coastline, where the diversity of plant, animal and insect life can be stunning. The seas, coves and surrounding hinterland has been a dramatic setting for a gloriously rich history, which have inspired countless tales of romance, drama and intrigue.

This series of Top Ten Walks explores highlights along the way; showcasing its natural beauty, wildlife and heritage and provoking imagination. Who knows, you may be inspired to come back to tackle the complete trail.

Fishing boats beached on the shingle at Beer, south Devon

The South Devon Coast

For many holiday-makers, Devon's south coast is synonymous with the vast sweep of Torbay, which can be almost Mediterranean in climate and offers some of the country's best loved holiday beaches. Yet there is so much more, its character constantly changing throughout its 130-mile length. Although only the section east of Exmouth is part of the Jurassic Coast World Heritage Site, much of the rest lies within the South Devon AONB. Few large conurbations infringe on its lavish beauty and abundant wildlife and flowers, a sense of history and the vivid revelation of geological formation serves to inspire.

"… the South Hams, which is famous for the best cider in that part of England "

Daniel Defoe, *London to Land's End*, 1724

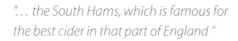

TOP 10 **Walks:** South Devon Coast

DEVON HAS BEEN DESCRIBED as one of England's most beautiful counties, its south coast encompassing everything from superb sandy beaches and soaring cliffs to secluded coves and sweeping bays. Meandering estuaries and narrow lanes wind to tiny villages and fishing settlements, where thatched cottages and perhaps a country pub cluster around an ancient church. The countryside is a patchwork of hedged fields, lush woodland and open down, all havens for wildlife and innumerable flowers. Here are the ten best walks to explore this glorious landscape.

Wembury Point — page 8

Bolt Tail & Bolberry Down — page 14

Bolt Head — page 18

Portlemouth Down — page 22

Prawle Point

Start Point

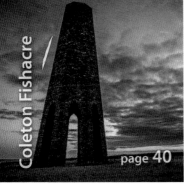

Coleton Fishacre

Otterton peninsula

Dunscombe Cliffs

Beer Head

St Werburgh's Church and Wembury Marine Centre above Wembury beach

Wembury Point

An easy yet interesting walk along the low cliffs flanking Wembury Point, with beaches and a grand little café

What to expect:
Field and coastal paths, old tracks and a short stretch on quiet lane

Distance/Time: 11 kilometres/ 7miles. Allow 3½ to 4 hours

Start: Wembury Beach National Trust car park (pay and display)

Grid ref: SX 517 484

Ordnance Survey map: Explorer OL20: South Devon

Refreshment: Eddystone Inn, Heybrook Bay | 01752 862572 | www.eddystoneinn.co.uk OR Old Mill Café, Wembury Beach | 01752 863280

Walk Outline

A pretty, wooded valley takes the walk inland from Wembury Bay, before climbing to higher ground beyond Home Farm. A short stretch of lane and fields lead over a low hill to Bovisand Lane. The old track heads down another delightful groove towards the coast at Bovisand Bay, where there is a lovely beach. Beyond Bovisand Holiday Centre, unspoiled low cliffs curve behind Heybrook Bay, leading pleasantly back to the beach and car park at Wembury Bay.

Wembury's wildlife

Wembury's coast has an amazing diversity of marine and terrestrial life and is protected by four separate conservation bodies. The rocky foreshore is ideal for exploring rock pools, where small fish, crustaceans and anemones can be found. Among the special plants here is the rare shore dock, which has narrower leaves than the more common variety and is usually found where freshwater seeps onto the beach. Call in at Wembury Marine Centre before beginning the walk for more in-depth information about the area's coastal wildlife.

Footbridge at Wembury

Beadlet anemone

The Walk

1. Drop left from the **car park** entrance past the **Old Mill Café** and swing right over a **bridge**. Immediately turn right again to follow a path inland by the **stream**. At the far end, bear right over **another bridge** to reach the lane. Go left to a junction. Cross to the drive opposite, but watch for the **bridleway** then branching off left along the lush valley.

2. Meeting a **narrow lane** at the end, go left to the bottom of the hill

and there take another **track** off right past **Higher Ford Farm**, the first of two adjacent drives. Briefly keep ahead at the top with a climbing path, but then fork left over a stile into the corner of a field.

Walk ahead across the slope to a stile at the far side and continue along the bottom edge from field to field. Passing through the corner of a **wood**, carry on, shortly joining a **grass track**. Stay with it as it then swings left through a gate, rising gently towards **Home Farm**. Before getting there, however, branch off right at a waypost and climb on beside an old, fragmented hedge on your left to a stile in the top corner.

The Great Mew Stone framed by the roof of St Werburgh's Church

Now turn right on a **field track**, following it within left the next corner to a stile in the high hedge. Strike out on a trod, aiming left of a **distant barn**. Reaching **Raneleigh Farm**, follow its track out left to a lane.

3. Turn right. At the next junction, cross to a signposted stile on the left into the corner of a field. Briefly follow the left hedge, veer right in front of an opening to head away from the lane, with a hedge still on your left. At a crossing path near the top of the field, swing right on a trod straight across the crop, which leads past an indented corner to a gate in the bottom corner. Carry on beside a line of derelict fence posts to emerge at the corner of a lane.

4. To the left, an old **hollow way** shrouded in trees, **Bovisand Lane**, heads gently down the valley, soon sharing its course with a babbling **brook**. Joining a track towards the bottom, keep going past a **caravan park**, but just beyond the entrance, bear off left with the old track again. A **small bay** opens ahead, with views of Bovisand Fort and the Plymouth Breakwater defences.

Plymouth Sound seen from the rocks in Bovisand Bay

5. Meeting the **Coast Path**, go left behind the bay and cross the stream. The way rises onto the **headland**, soon joining a drive past the chalets of **Bovisand Holiday Centre**. Keep going past a parking area, where there is access to the beach. Eventually the drive swings right past more parking towards the coast.

6. At the end of the drive, branch left to **Heybrook Bay**.

Undulate on above low cliffs overlooking a rocky, tide-washed platform. Further on, are the **remnants of wartime installations**. Rounding the point behind **Renney Rocks**, the **Great Mew Stone**

comes into view. Houses herald your arrival at **Heybrook Bay**, the path joining a track out to a lane.

7. Bear right across **Hey Brook**. Keep ahead at a signpost up a drive past the last houses to branch right with the **Coast Path** around **Wembury Point**.

Throughout the 19th century, growth in trade fuelled expansion at Britain's ports; however, Plymouth's development was hampered by its naval presence. Instead a new commercial port was ambitiously conceived for Wembury Bay, but lack of investment and isolation from the railway brought the plans to nought.

The interwar years saw the popularity of

'holiday camps' rise, two opening here offering accommodation in wooden chalets. Wembury Point was quite commercialised, boasting a roller skating rink on the clubhouse roof. Patches, however, was more refined with a sea-water swimming pool, but it was requisitioned during World War Two as part of HMS Cambridge, a naval gunnery school.

Continue back to **Wembury Bay** to complete the walk. ◆

The Great Mew Stone

Now a nature reserve, the distinctively shaped offshore island is an important breeding site for shags, cormorants and other sea birds. During the 18th and 19th centuries, it was inhabited, initially by a local man who in 1744 was sentenced to seven years' banishment there for a petty crime. He chose to stay on after his term and the island remained occupied until the last occupant was arrested for smuggling.

Looking towards Bolt Tail from from Bolberry Down

Bolt Tail & Bolberry Down

A relatively simple but rewarding walk exploring the impressive cliffs of Bolt Tail

What to expect:
Field and coastal paths, some lane walking

Distance/Time: 7.5 kilometres/ 4¾ miles. Allow 2¾ to 3¼ hours

Start: Bolberry Down National Trust car park (pay and display)

Grid ref: SX 689 384

Ordnance Survey map: Explorer OL20: South Devon

Refreshments: The Sun Bay Hotel at Hope Cove | 01548 561371 | www.sunbayhotel-hopecove.co.uk OR Ocean's Restaurant, Bolberry Down | 01548 562467 | www.oceansrestaurant.co.uk

Walk outline

Beginning from the coastal car park, the route heads back inland through Bolberry before taking to field paths and tracks to regain the coast at Hope Cove. There is an opportunity to spend time on the fine beach before climbing away onto Bolt Tail, where the promontory tip lies behind an impressive prehistoric ditch and rampart. The way returns along the grassy cliff top, passing impressive rocks and ongoing coastal slump before returning across Bolberry Down to the car park.

Ancient Man on Bolberry Down

Finds of flint scrapers, arrowheads and other stone tools suggest that Man has been wandering these downs for at least 6,000 years. More obvious evidence of his presence lies in the impressive ditch and rampart that runs across the neck of Bolt Tail. It is thought to date from around 600BC, built by the *Dumnonii*, a Celtic Iron Age tribe. Commonly called a promontory fort, it was certainly well defended, with sheer cliffs on three sides and a formidable wall facing the land, but archaeologists still debate how such structures were used.

Cottages, Inner Hope

Honeysuckle

The Walk

1. From the car park, follow the lane back over the hill to **Bolberry**. At the bottom, go left and then, in a few metres, fork off right down a **narrower lane**. Beyond **cottages**, climb away, the lane shortly swinging sharp right.

2. Leave at that point along an **old hollow way**, romantically called **Sweethearts Lane**. Emerging onto a **track** opposite a converted barn, go left. Approaching gates to another house, turn off right on a climbing path signed towards 'Galmpton'. Walk up to a stile and bear left on a trod across a meadow to find a gate in the top boundary. Entering the corner of a crop field, the path runs to the right beside the hedge.

3. Through a gate at the top, turn left through a second gate and walk on along a field-edge track. The village across the valley is Galmpton. Gently losing height, the coast soon comes into view ahead, Burgh Island a prominent feature before **Hope** appears in sight. Leaving the cultivation, the path continues beside grassland, later joining a track past houses to meet a lane.

4. Take the path opposite, descending steps past **St Clement's Church** to come out onto a lower lane. The main beach is to the right along the **South West Coast Path**, but the route continues to the left. Keep right at a junction in front of the **Sun Bay Hotel** and walk down to the **lifeboat house** and **slipway**.

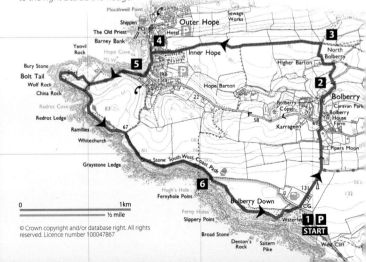

The South West Coast Path approaching Hope

5. Pass in front of the **boathouse** and follow the **Coast Path** up steps into **woodland** cloaking the headland's lower slope. Breaking from the trees, the way dips across the open down, rising to a gap in the **Iron Age rampart**. Beyond, bear off right to reach the rocky tip of **Bolt Tail**.

Carry on around the coast, sweeping in behind the sheer cliffs to re-cross the ancient bank above **Redrot Cove**. The way undulates on at the edge of the down, with occasional waymarks.

6. Through a gate, join a formal path, branching right at the next fork. The car park soon comes into sight and the path turns inland. However, keep ahead to find a **rocky viewpoint above Waterfern**. A path then skirts its edge back to the car park to complete the walk. ♦

Wildlife on Bolberry Down
The area is a designated Site of Special Scientific Interest (SSSI) for its special range of plants, which attract birds and insects. Listen for skylarks and look out for stonechats or even Dartford warblers. Mining bees and the rare short-necked oil beetle are among the insects to be seen and there are slow worms here too. Still more curious is dodder, a parasitic plant growing on the gorse and covering it in orange hair-like tendrils.

Looking back into Salcombe harbour from the rocks on Bolt Head

Bolt Head

Grand cliff scenery at Sharp Tor and Bolt Head, and chance to visit National Trust house and gardens at Overbeck's

What to expect:
Field tracks, woodland and cliff paths, one sustained climb

Distance/Time: 7 kilometres/ 4½ miles. Allow 2½ to 3 hours

Start: Middle Soar National Trust car park, Soar

Grid ref: SX 713 375

Ordnance Survey map: Explorer OL20: South Devon

Refreshments: South Sands Hotel, South Sands, Salcombe | 01548 845900 | www.southsands.com

Walk Outline

After heading east along a track from the car park, the way continues over fields before turning into Tor Woods. A permissive path winds across tree clad slopes, to emerge below Overbeck's. A track heads for the coast, opening onto the cliffs to head around the craggy tip of Sharp Tor. There is then a climb from Starehole Bottom onto Bolt Head, beyond which the path remains high before crossing The Warren to pick up a track past Middle Soar back to the car park.

Sharp Tor topograph

RAF Bolt Head

Even as the last of the harvest left the fields, engineers moved in to grub out hedges and roll down matting runways; such was the urgency in 1940 to mobilise fighter escorts to defend bombers heading across the Channel. Solid buildings soon replaced tents and the base operated around the clock. Air Sea Rescue was also stationed here and, in 1941, a Ground Control Interceptor station was added to direct fighters to their targets. The station finally closed in 1947 and the fields returned to farming, but for a period during the Cold War, it was the site of a radar station and nuclear bunker.

Clouded yellow butterfly

The Walk

1. Leave the **car park** through a gate by the **information boards** on a broad track between the fields. Where it later bends right, keep ahead through a gate, signed to 'Tor Woods and Overbeck's'. Continue across a field, a trod guiding you to a small gate in the far left corner. Walk on by the left hedge bank in the next long field to reach another gate and signpost.

2. Go left at the edge of a small field to enter **Tor Woods**. Take the path off left, which initially loses height near the top edge of the trees. Later reaching a signpost, go sharp right towards Overbeck's and Salcombe, now dropping through the heart of the wood. Lower down, watch for a fork and branch up

right, shortly emerging onto a lane. The entrance to **Overbeck's house and garden** is then up to the right.

3. The onward route, however, is down the hill. Rounding a sharp bend, take a **wooded track** off on the right signed as the South West Coast Path to 'Starehole'. Beyond a gate, the way diminishes to a path, the trees later thinning to open up views across the estuary towards Portlemouth Down. Ahead are the dramatic craggy rocks of **Sharp Tor**, the path shortly stepped and railed as it passes around the outcrop and on along the cliffs before descending to **Starehole Cove**.

4. Through a gate, continue ahead towards **Bolt Head**, the path rising in a steady, stiff pull onto the headland. The climb is rewarded by striking views back across Starehole Bay and in the other direction towards the distant Cornish coast. Below, the sea crashes against the offshore stacks of the **Mew Stones**. Stick with the

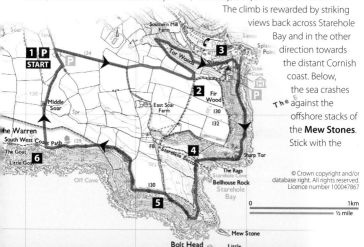

0   1km

0   ½ mile

Starehole Cove framed by yellow gorse in summer

continuing **Coast Path** off the head, bearing left towards a gate in a wall.

5. The onward path, signed to 'Soar Mill Cove' runs easily across gorse-covered downland, later passing through a gate and leading to a second gate and signpost above **Off Cove**. Take the left fork, which continues across the gorse, shortly leading to yet another signpost.

6. There, turn right towards 'Marlborough', crossing pasture to a gate in a wall. Keep going to the **farmhouse at Middle Soar**, the path skirting its gardens on the right through successive gates. Follow the drive away to emerge by a **cattle grid** onto a track. Turn left and walk back to the **car park** to complete the walk. ♦

Overbeck's

Overbeck's was the home of inventor Otto Overbeck. His greatest success was the 'Rejuvenator', an electrical therapy machine that he claimed could cure all sorts of ailments and halt the aging process. Otto supported his electrode theory with books on the 'electrical theory of life', which, he claimed, made religion redundant. His invention made him rich, and he used part of his fortune to buy the property, bequeathing it to the National Trust on his death in 1937.

The ferry leaving East Portlemouth for Salcombe

Portlemouth Down

A pleasing walk featuring a curious lookout and an optional ferry crossing of one of the coast's many estuaries

What to expect:
Woodland tracks, undulating coastal path and quiet lanes

Distance/Time: 8 kilometres/ 5 miles. Allow 2½ to 3 hours

Start: Creek car park, Salcombe (pay and display); alternative start for shorter walk, Mill Bay National Trust car park (pay and display)

Grid refs: SX 739 393, (Salcombe) SX 743 380 (National Trust car park)

Ordnance Survey map: Explorer OL20: South Devon

Refreshments: The Ferry Inn, Salcombe | 01548 844000 | www.theferryinnsalcombe.com OR Gara Rock Hotel | 03333 700555 | www.gararock.com

Walk Outline

Start by walking through Salcombe to the ferry and cross the harbour to the eastern bank. Continue along a lane to Mill Bay, where the way turns inland behind Portlemouth Down. A steady climb along a wooded valley leads over the hill to Gara Rock. Below a curious thatched lookout, the route joins the South West Coast Path to undulate above the sloping cliffs back to Mill Bay. From there the way retraces the lane to the ferry.

Thatched lookout station

Salcombe

Despite its sheltered position within a long tidal estuary, for much of its history Salcombe remained merely a tiny fishing village. Even in the 17th century, it was at risk from Barbary pirates plundering coastal settlements and seizing captives for the North African slave trade. There was further disruption during the Civil War, when Royalists refurbished the Tudor castle. But the 19th century brought prosperity, with shipbuilding yards around the coast. When tourists started to arrive, they set a fashion that continues today.

Bloody cranesbill

The Walk

1. Leaving **Creek long stay car park**, walk left towards the town. At the end of the street, turn left along **Shadycombe Road**, going left again at the next junction into **Church Street**. Follow it around successive bends, eventually swinging right along **Fore Street**. Carry on to the next bend and leave down steps to the **ferry**.

During the Second World War, Salcombe was one of many places along the coast where secret preparations and training were undertaken in advance of the D Day landings on 6th June 1944. British and American troops and amphibious landing craft assembled in Salcombe before crossing the Channel as part of the landing force headed for the Utah beaches in Normandy. A lucky combination of circumstances meant that, although landing a mile off their intended target, they encountered less resistance than anticipated and suffered fewer casualties in securing their objectives than their comrades on other beaches.

2. Alighting on the estuary's far bank, climb to the street above and follow it right for 800 metres to the **National Trust car park at Mill Bay**.

The tranquil coastline at Gara Rock bay

3. Turn left, the way signed to 'Rickham'. Passing through a gate at the far end of the car park, a wooded path rises gently along the valley. Emerging onto a lane, cross to the continuing path opposite, signed to 'Gara Rock'. The trees are soon left behind, the way now contained between fields. Keep going across a final field to come out onto a drive, which to the right leads to the **Gara Rock Hotel**.

4. Walk past the complex, the way then swinging left and narrowing to a path. Immediately, a path off right leads to a whitewashed, **thatched lookout**, hidden behind the outcrop of rock.

Originally built as part of a Coastguard Station, whose original cottages have now been subsumed within the Gara Rock Hotel, it commands an excellent view along the coast. Over to the east on the sloping valley side, the ridges of ancient field boundaries can be seen, reckoned to be perhaps 3,000 years old. There are also the remains of hut platforms — part of a small settlement.

Return to the main path and continue right, dropping to a junction. Go right, signed to 'Mill Bay' and follow the path as it curves back below the lookout, falling beyond to meet the **South West**

Looking across the estuary to Salcombe from East Portlemouth

Coast Path. Turn right to pass another **viewpoint** and then walk round a corner to a fork.

Over a period from 1977, occasional underwater finds of small copper ingots and other artefacts led to the discovery of a Bronze Age shipwreck below the cliffs. Dated to around 900 BC it is the oldest of only a handful of such known sites dotted around the British coast. In addition to a sword, other weaponry and gold jewellery, over 290 small ingots of copper and 27 ingots of tin have been recovered. The copper, from Spain, together with tin, possibly Cornish, are the constituent elements for bronze and indicate an extensive and sophisticated trade network. Built of wood, the sea-going vessel has not survived, but experts believe it was probably around 6 feet wide and 40 feet long.

5. Branch left with the lower path, which undulates easily across the steep gorse slope of the coast. *There are impressive views in both directions, that ahead across the mouth of the estuary. As you approach the mouth of the inlet, the vista opens along the beaches and bays opposite.*

Ignore paths climbing inland and carry on around the point to a signposted junction of paths beside a **memorial to the Salcombe Lifeboat disaster**.

6. Keep with the **Coast Path** around **Limebury Point**, dropping back into a woodland of twisted sycamore and oak, and eventually returning to the junction at the entrance to the **National Trust car park** (**3**). As an alternative to retracing your outward route to the ferry, if the tide is safely out, you can instead walk along the beach.

From the landing, take the **ferry** back to **Salcombe** to complete the walk. ♦

Salcombe Lifeboat Disaster

On 27 October 1916, Salcombe's lifeboat, the William and Emma *was returning home, having been called to help the* Western Lass, *foundering off Prawle Point. Amidst hurricane force winds, the crew tried to row into the estuary, but treacherous waves, created by an underwater sandbar across the mouth, capsized the boat and all but two of the fifteen-man crew were lost in what was one of the worst disasters in lifeboat history.*

On the South West Coast Path overlooking Prawle Point

Prawle Point

A largely undemanding walk combining the dramatic scenery of Prawle Point with a gentler coastline to the east

What to expect:
A rocky coast path, some lane and old tracks, a steady climb towards the end

Distance/Time: 7 kilometres/ 4¼ miles. Allow 2¼ to 3¾ hours

Start: East Prawle, park around village green (donation)

Grid ref: SX 780 363

Ordnance Survey map: Explorer OL20: South Devon

Refreshments: Pig Nose Inn, East Prawle | 01548 511209 | www.pigsnoseinn.co.uk, OR Piglet Café, East Prawle | 01548 511486

Walk Outline

Starting from Prawle's attractive green, the walk leaves the village along a quiet lane before branching off on an old track across the hillside. There's a view to the west as the route turns toward the coast to join the South West Coast Path above Gammon Head. After sweeping high behind sandy coves, the path rises to Prawle Point, where there is a National Coastwatch station and exhibition. Falling past former station cottages, the way continues above an apron of rock before turning inland above Horseley Cove to climb back to East Prawle.

Prawle Point

The headland is the southernmost tip of Devon and the hilltop was the site of an Admiralty signal station during the Napoleonic Wars. The present lookout was established in 1860 with cottages later built to house the watchkeepers. It has served the Coastguard as well as relaying ship to shore signals for the both the Navy and Lloyds in the days before radio. The area is notoriously dangerous for shipping, and with the help of the Prawle Rescue Team, many lives have been saved using rocket line and breeches buoy to bring crews ashore.

National Coastwatch station

Cirl bunting

The Walk

1. Take the ongoing lane from the top of the green, signed to 'Prawle Point'.

2. Where it later bends sharply left, leave ahead on a **bridleway**, which undulates gently between flower-rich banks. At the end, there is a fine view over a gate along the coast west towards Bolt Head. Turn left before it towards the craggy spine of **Gammon Head**. Reaching a junction, keep right, dropping to meet the **South West Coast Path**, which descends from the headland.

3. To the left the way winds behind **Elender Cove** and **Black Cove**, becoming rocky and rising more steeply towards **Prawle Point**. Cresting the rise, there is a grand vista in all directions, the impressive cliffs of Gammon Head contrasting with a long run of low-tide reefs to the east.

Wreckage stranded on the rocks below, with more visible just out to sea, is all that remains of the Demetrius, *which foundered during a storm in December 1992. Ironically it was under tow from Dunkirk to a breakers' yard in the Mediterranean when the cable*

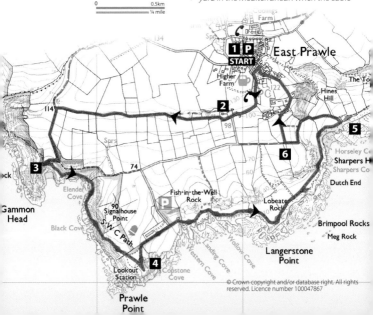

The South West Coast Path as it heads for for Prawle Point

parted and she was helplessly driven onto the rocks. The stricken hulk was a local attraction for several weeks before what was left could be salvaged for scrap.

Carry on, passing a curious **row of upturned slabs**, part of an ancient field boundary.

Old English for lookout, Prawle Point is Devon's southernmost headland, and has been a vantage down the centuries. A long-gone medieval chapel dedicated to Brendan, the Irish saint who reputedly sailed the Atlantic in search of an island Paradise, would have been a welcome landmark for seafarers, while around 1799, a semaphore signal station was established, part of a country-wide system that transmitted messages between naval shipping and the Admiralty in London. The Coastguard established a station in 1860, which then also served to report early news of returning vessels to owners and insurers at Lloyd's in London and the start of the 20th century saw the establishment of a Naval Signal Shore Station, with the nearby cottages housing the crew. Developing technology gradually replaced its several functions

Looking down on Langerstone Point from the lookout station on Prawle Point

and it was finally decommissioned in 1994, only to be re-opened three years later as a NCI lookout, which provides a volunteer daytime watch throughout the year.

4. Turn in from the cliffs, now heading towards the **Coastguard cottage**s and falling to a gate. Continue at the field edge below their gardens, passing through more gates beyond as the path closes with the coast once more.

The overgrown **wartime bunkers** *housed a radar station to give early warning of approaching enemy aircraft.* The **Coast Path** winds above low cliffs past **Langerstone Point**, where there is

access to the shore, and on to **Horseley Cove**.

5. Meeting a track from the beach, follow it left a short distance to a second junction and there keep ahead with the ongoing **bridleway** between fields, signed to 'East Prawle'.

Carry on beyond a gate, the way gaining height from the coast past a fringe of **woodland**. Higher up, follow the track around a sharp right-hand bend.

6. At a junction, go right and continue climbing to come out onto a lane beside a **cottage**. Follow it right, still uphill, to return to the village, passing the **Pigs**

Nose Inn on the edge of the green, to complete the walk. ♦

During the Second World War, the pub was popular with RAF servicemen manning navigation and early warning stations at Gee and Chain Home Low, above West Prawle — navigation and early warning systems to assist British bombers and detect approaching enemy aircraft. The radar remained until 1954 .

Anti-submarine patrols

During the First World War, the main threat to coastal shipping was from enemy submarines. In 1917, to support the work of the shore-based watch station, a Royal Naval Air Station was established on a grass airfield outside East Prawle, which undertook anti-submarine patrols along the Channel. It became RAF Prawle Point when the Royal Air Force was created the following year and remained in operation until early 1919.

Late evening sunlight illuminates the lighthouse at Start Point

Start Point

A more strenuous walk to one of England's most exposed peninsulas and a storm-ruined fishing village

What to expect:
Undulating coast paths, farm tracks and some quiet lane, with a couple of steeper ascents

Distance/Time: 11.5 kilometres/ 7¼ miles. Allow 4 to 4½ hours

Start: Hallsands car park, Bickerton, alternative start at Start Point car park (charge)

Grid ref: SX 817 388 (Hallsands), SX 820 375 (Start Point)

Ordnance Survey map: Explorer OL20: South Devon

Refreshment: Nearest pub – The Cricket Inn, Beesands | 01548 580 215 | www.thecricketinn.com

Walk Outline

Leaving the beach at Hallsands, the route follows steep, quiet lanes over the hill into neighbouring Lannacombe valley. Another stiff climb leads to easy field tracks over the tops to Borough and then a gentle descent to the South West Coast Path at Woodcombe. The way continues above low cliffs, offering opportunities to reach the shore before a final pull onto the Start Point peninsula. After an optional diversion to the lighthouse, return across coastal slopes to Hallsands.

A lost village

Tucked below the cliffs, old Hallsands was a small but lively fishing village centred around its pub, the London Inn. With no harbour, the fishing boats were drawn up onto the shingle. However, when offshore dredging to provide material for the expansion of the naval dockyard at Keyham began in 1890s, the beach began to subside alarmingly, threatening the homes. Only after two enquiries was dredging finally stopped. Yet the damage had already been done. Winter storms took their toll until, in January 1917, almost every house was washed away.

South West Coast Path sign

Atlantic grey seal

Looking back along the shore at Hallsands towards Start Point

The Walk

1. Leave the southern end of the **car park**, turning right up steps towards 'Start Point'. The way joins a lane past **Prospect House**, opposite which is a **viewpoint** and **interpretation panel** overlooking the site of **Hallsands lost village**. Carry on up the lane for 800 metres, keeping left at a junction to reach a cross-road.

Over to the left on the high point of the peninsula rise the twin masts of the Start Point radio transmitter. It was one of two established by the BBC in 1935 (the other, also still operating was at Clevedon in Somerset) to improve radio reception for the early Regional Programme service to the west of England. It operated until 1939, closing down just two days before the outbreak of the Second World War to prevent its use as a navigation beacon by enemy aircraft. By 1940, advancing technology allowed the station to safely re-open carrying the newly formed Home Service as well as the Forces' Programme and a European service. Normal service resumed after the war and continues today with medium wave transmissions of Radio 5 Live.*

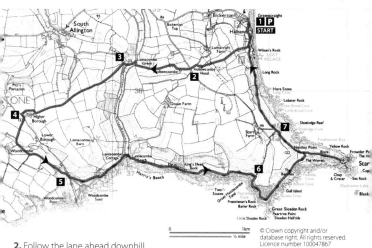

© Crown copyright and/or database right. All rights reserved. Licence number 100047867

2. Follow the lane ahead downhill towards 'Lannacombe'. At the bottom, take the second left. Walk past a **cottage** and then look for a bridleway signed off sharp left to 'East Prawle'.

3. Immediately through the gate, disregard the path ahead and instead, go right and then left onto a higher path. Shortly breaking from trees, the route climbs steeply across open, rough meadow. Through a gate at the top, bear right to find another gate at the end of a farm track. The way ahead runs easily over the hill towards **Higher Borough**. Approaching the farm, the track swings right and then left past a junction.

4. At the end, go left again, but then, almost opposite the main entrance to the farm, turn off right on a bridleway.

After some 400 metres, approaching barns at **Woodcombe**, leave through a gate on the left. Walk away past a **pond**, making for another gate at the top of the field. Go right to a wooden gate onto a hedged track and follow it left, eventually reaching a junction with the **South West Coast Path**.

5. Follow it left towards Lannacombe, passing a path signed off down to Ivy Cove. At **Lannacombe**, the way briefly joins the lane past a **small car park** above the beach, before continuing towards Start Point above low cliffs along **The Narrows**. There is another access to the shore at **Great Mattiscombe Sand** and a path inland, which bypasses the headland, should you need it.

The last rays of the sun catch Start Point lighthouse at dusk

Looking across the narrowing English Channel towards Guernsey and France, Start Point oversees the busiest shipping lane in the world, with some 500 ships passing through each day. Radar, traffic control and GPS systems have dramatically reduced the number of accidents, but historically the picture was very different with shipwreck and tragic loss of life being all-too frequent. The worst disaster off Start Point was in 1891 when, on the 9th March, two ships came aground during the Great Blizzard. The first to hit the rocks was the SS Marana, a schooner rigged steamer en route from London to Columbo in Ceylon (Sri Lanka) carrying a cargo of telegraph poles and sleepers. Of the 28 crew members only five made it ashore, with two of those subsequently dying from exposure as the lifeboat had overturned. Hours later, the SV Dryad, which had left Tyneside six days before bound for Valpariso carrying mining equipment and coal, foundered against the cliffs nearby. None of the 21-man crew survived, although one managed to make it onto the rocks but froze to death before help arrived. .

6. The walk, however, remains with the **Coast Path** around the headland, soon bringing the lighthouse into view. The way climbs across the steep slope to crest the spine of the **narrow peninsula**

of Start Point, dropping to a tarmac track beyond. The lighthouse is then some 400 metres to the right at the end of the track, but the way back lies to the left, climbing to a **cliff-top car park**.

7. Across the car park, bear right with the **Coast Path**, which drops across the cliffs towards **Hallsands**. Emerging on a lane by **Prospect House**, turn right and retrace your steps back to the **car park at Hallsands Beach** to complete the walk. ♦

Start Point Lighthouse

Built in 1836 and perched on the edge of the cliff, the Start Point light marks the end of a long peninsula and dangerous offshore rocks that protrude into the English Channel. The site is not immune to erosion and in 1989 the fog signal building collapsed, requiring a new one to be constructed. The station has been automated since 1993 but is open for guided tours on Sundays and other selected days during the summer.

'The Tower' is a lofty 'daymark' or navigation beacon

Coleton Fishacre

Wooded coves, cliff-top views and wartime ruins, passing Coleton Fishacre, the one-time home of the D'Oyly Cartes

What to expect:
*Good tracks and an un-
dulating cliff path with
some steeper sections*

Distance/Time: 11 kilometres/ 7 miles. Allow 3½ to 4 hours

Start: Coleton Camp National Trust car park (honesty box)

Grid ref: SX 909 512

Ordnance Survey map: Explorer OL20: South Devon

Refreshments: Coleton Fishacre licensed café (National Trust) | 01803 842382 | www.nationaltrust.org.uk/coleton-fishacre

Walk Outline

The first leg runs beside fields to the coast at Scabbacombe Head. The coastal section meanders past the foot of Coleton Fishacre and around Froward Point, where an exhibition of local wildlife, history and wartime activity is housed. After dropping to Mill Bay Cove, where there is access to the beach, the way winds inland to Brownstone Farm and wanders out to The Tower, a conspicuous navigation marker. The final stretch follows a lane back to the car park.

Coleton Fishacre

Built in the early 1920s, Coleton Fishacre and its lovely gardens that flow from the house down a secluded valley to a sheltered cove, was home to the D'Oyly Cartes. The family ran the Savoy Hotel and their own opera company, famous for its productions of Gilbert and Sullivan's comic operas. The house, designed by Oswald Mine, who briefly worked with Sir Edward Lutyens before setting up his own architectural practice, harks back to the Arts and Crafts movement, but its decoration and fittings largely reflect the then contemporary Art Deco style.

Kingswear Castle

Small pearl-bordered fritillary

The Walk

1. Leave the **car park** by the **information board**, walking along the top of a **picnic area**. Through a gate in the corner, join a track heading left towards 'Scabbacombe Head'. Beyond a small gate at the end, carry on beside fields, finally dropping through a second gate to a junction.

2. It is worth walking left a little way for views across Scabbacombe Sands. The onward route, however, is to the right around **Scabbacombe Head**. Joining the **South West Coast Path**, which shortly rises from the left, wind around the head of a **gully** and continue to **Ivy Cove**.

3. Ignore the inland path (back to the car park) and carry on, remaining high through bracken and gorse. The view ahead is to the Mew Stone and its satellites off Outer Froward Point, but closer to, the path turns in behind **Pudcombe Cove**, falling to cross a **stream** at the head. Thickly wooded, the cove lies at the foot of the **National Trust's Coleton Fishacre estate**, the once accessible beach having a small **swimming pool** cut into the rock.

Coleton Fishacre was once the home of the D'Oyly Carte family

4. Immediately over a **bridge**, go left past a **viewpoint** before winding steeply up through the **woods** to regain the **cliff top**. Further on the way dips again around the heads of **Old Mill Bay** and **Froward Cove** before rising to a gate into open **woodland**, where ponies often graze. Where the path forks take either. The lower branch drops along the cliffs before climbing past the remains of Second World War **gun emplacements**, part of the **Brownstone Battery**. The other remains high, leading past an **overgrown bunker** to a tarmac drive.

Follow that left to the **battery buildings**, one housing a **small visitor centre** while another serves as a **National Coastwatch station**.

Brownstone's Second World War gun battery, established in 1940 to defend against coastal invasion, is one of a few to have survived largely intact. It includes the observation and command post and other buildings used to house ammunition, stores and the men who manned the post. The twin gun emplacements, searchlight positions and one of the generator buildings also remain.

Overlooking the sea from the South West Coast Path near Coleton Fishacre

5. Dropping past the top corner of another building, the onward **Coast Path** is signed to 'Kingswear'. After undulating through **The Warren**, the way eventually leaves the Brownstone estate. Ignoring private paths, the route continues through woodland, eventually dropping steeply into the foot of the valley to emerge onto a drive by a **castellated folly** overlooking **Mill Bay Cove**.

6. Go right, but just before a **cattle grid**, turn off left with the continuing **Coast Path**. Beyond a **stream** and gate, there is access to the **tiny beach**, otherwise carry on, climbing through the woods, across

a **private drive** and finally up **steps** to reach a lane.

7. Walk right, taking the lower fork where it later splits, and drop to the end of the track by a red **telephone box** at **Home Farm**. Go right, climbing an old **sunken way** to emerge onto the end of a drive by **holiday cottages**. Carry on to **Higher Brownstone**, passing the farm to reach a junction.

8. Turn off right on a **farm track**, signed as a link to the 'Coast Path'. Climbing to a junction, keep right again, winding between fields towards the towering

Daymark. Standing within a field, it is accessed through a gate.

9. Return to the last junction and now go right, sticking with the track as it later winds left. Just before its end, turn off right on a path parallel to a lane. Walking through a **car park**, continue along the lane past **Coleton Farm** to a junction by the **entrance to Coleton Fishacre**. Keep ahead to return to the **Coleton Camp car park**, to complete the walk. ♦

The Daymark

Impressive from afar and distinctly odd close to, this novel structure is a navigation tower. In essence, a lighthouse without a light, it was built in 1864 by the Dartmouth Harbour Commissioners to help guide shipping into the harbour, sheltered deep within the narrow Dart estuary. Hollow inside and without a roof, the 25-metre octagonal structure rises elegantly above the headland on eight arched legs and, in clear weather, is visible from over 20 miles away.

A picturesque group of Scots pines at the mouth of the River Otter

Otterton Peninsula

A relatively easy walk through a riverside nature reserve, an attractive village and along fine cliffs

What to expect:
Good riverside paths, undulating cliff tops and village lanes

Distance/Time: 12 kilometres/ 7½ miles. Allow 3¼ to 3¾ hours

Start: Lime Kiln car park, Budleigh Salterton

Grid ref: SY 072 820

Ordnance Survey map: Explorer 115: Exmouth & Sidmouth

Refreshment: Kings Arms, Otterton | 01395 568416| www.kingsarmsotterton.co.uk, also pubs and cafes in Sidmouth

Walk Outline

Beginning above Salterton Beach, the walk traces the River Otter to the ancient village of Otterton. Old lanes take the way on to the coastal cliffs above Chiselbury Bay from which the return follows a long run of gently undulating cliffs back to the River Otter's estuary. With no way across the river mouth, the path turns upstream in search of a crossing, finally retracing the outward route back to the start.

Budleigh Salterton

Originally a farming and fishing village that grew around ancient salt pans beside the Otter estuary, it was a childhood haunt of the Elizabethan soldier, courtier and explorer Sir Walter Raleigh, who was born nearby at Hayes Barton. Indeed, Sir John Everett Millais came here to paint his famous picture *The Boyhood of Raleigh*, which has as a backdrop, the town's sea wall, which still stands today. The arrival of the railway and the Victorian passion for sea bathing gave Budleigh a new lease of life as a holiday resort during the latter part of the 19th century.

Otterton village sign

Otter

The Walk

1. Head upstream beside the **Otter estuary** along a **gravel path**, which leaves the top-right corner of the car park. Crossing a lane by a **bridge**, stay beside the river, eventually meeting the bend of a track. Bear right to cross a side **stream**, shortly passing by a **second bridge** and ultimately emerging onto a lane.

The river was once navigable, enabling the Saxon settlement of Otterton to develop as a small but thriving port. Boats brought in wine, fish and other goods, leaving with cargoes of wool bound for the Continent, a lucrative trade that brought prosperity to the town.

However, by the beginning of the 16th century, gradual silting, not helped by a shingle bank forming across the estuary, prevented all but the smallest craft travelling upriver. Trade shifted to Ottermouth, where fishing, salt pans, boat building and lime kilns were important activities. During the 19th century, Napoleonic prisoners of war were employed in raising a bank to contain the river and reclaim land for pasture; the path underfoot follows its course.

The White Bridge on the River Otter near Otterton

The estuary and lower valley encompass a range of different habitats including shingle bank, salt marsh, reed bed, water meadow, wet woodland and of course the river itself. This in turn attracts a host of wildlife and flora that changes throughout the year.

The bridges give a good view into the clear water where the fish include trout, grey mullet and even salmon. Birds you might spot are kingfisher, little egret, reed and sedge warblers and reed bunting, while in winter there are waders such as widgeon, curlew and redshank. Butterflies flit amongst the flowers and dragonflies are

often to be seen too. Amongst the plants, look for meadowsweet and tansy, long known for their medicinal properties and scurvy grass, so called because it helped keep sailors healthy during long voyages.

2. Turn right across the **river** into **Otterton**, passing an **old mill** that has been restored to incorporate a bakery and craft shop. Carry on past the **King's Arms** towards the far end of the village.

3. Reaching a junction, turn off right along **Lea Road**. At the end, go left and then almost immediately right on a rising track signed as an unmetalled road. It

Otter Head at the mouth of the River Otter, near Budleigh Salterton

soon levels off, passes a junction and then turns abruptly left. Keep with it to meet a lane at the end.

4. Go left, walking up to a **small green**. There, leave right on a metalled drive. Reaching the entrance to **Monks Wall**, bear right with the footpath, which leads into the corner of a field. Walk on beside the righthand boundary to meet the coast near **Smallstones Point**.

5. At the shallow corner, turn through a kissing gate on the right and follow the **South West Coast Path** towards Budleigh Salterton, in time passing **Brandy Head**, the highest point along

this stretch of cliff and the site of a **Second World War observation post**.

The area was used by the RAF for airborne gunnery training and weapons and gunsight development. From their base at Exeter, pilots would fly out to shoot at targets positioned in the bay below and even on the land behind. Their success or otherwise was monitored from the reinforced cliff-top lookout.

6. Eventually approaching the **mouth of the River Otter**, the path turns inland past an impressive stand of pine. Glimpses through the trees reveal the estuary to be all but blocked by a shingle

bar holding back tidal pools and mud flats. A short distance on, a path branches off and leads through the trees to a bird hide. However, the route carries on, soon joining a track from **South Farm**.

7. Bend left past a junction to cross the **River Otter**. Immediately over the **bridge**, turn left along the riverside path, retracing your steps back to the car park to complete the walk. ♦

Beavers back in Britain

Although named for otters, the river is now home to beavers. Hunted to extinction in Britain during the 18th century, native Eurasian beavers were first spotted on the river here in 2008. Their origin is a mystery, but there are now eight family groups within the catchment. Their activities contribute to the diversity of habitats along the river and close monitoring and management ensures that dam building does not cause detrimental flooding.

Looking eastwards from Higher Dunscombe Cliff towards Weston Mouth

Dunscombe Cliffs

Enjoy deep, wooded combes and stunning clifftop scenery, along with Devon's famous Donkey Sanctuary

What to expect:
Generally clear paths with occasional steep ups and downs in the combes

Distance/Time: 9.5 kilometres/ 6 miles. Allow 3½ to 4 hours

Start: Salcombe Hill National Trust car park

Grid ref: SY 139 881

Ordnance Survey map: Explorer 115: Exmouth & Sidmouth

Refreshment: The Kitchen at The Donkey Sanctuary | 01395 578222 | www.thedonkeysanctuary.org.uk

Walk Outline
Beginning from a small National Trust woodland car park, the route dips around the head of the Salcombe valley before crossing fields to Dunscombe. A little more field walking leads to the Donkey Sanctuary, where a visitor centre and café give an opportunity for a break. The way then drops along pretty Weston Combe. There's access to the beach at both Weston and Salcombe mouths as the way then follows the South West Coast Path back to Salcombe Hill.

The Donkey Sanctuary
The Devon Donkey Sanctuary at Weston was founded as a small centre in 1969 by Dr Elizabeth Svendson to rescue and care for the well-being of working donkeys and mules. It has since developed into a world-wide charity, helping communities across the globe that rely on working donkeys for their livelihood as well as providing riding therapy to thousands of children. The sanctuary is open every day with free admission and you are invited to look around.

Donkey sanctuary

Common rock rose

The Walk

1. Leave the bottom left corner of the **car park** to head away along a track.

Norman Lockyer was a scientist and astronomer who retired to Salcombe Regis, where he founded an astronomical observatory, which stands across the lane from the car park. Lockyer was interested in electromagnetic spectroscopy and the sun; in 1868, this led him to identify helium, a gas not previously known on earth. He also established the scientific journal Nature. He died in 1920 and is buried in the village churchyard.

Approaching a gate, turn off left and follow a path within the **edge of the wood**. Towards the end, fork right to a crossing and take the path opposite, signed to 'Salcombe Regis', which slants down across the valley-side through the trees.

2. Meeting a **narrow lane** at the end, go right towards **Combe Wood Farm**. Keep ahead at the end between buildings to a gate, through which immediately branch left on a rising path. At the top, go left to find a **kissing gate** on the right and walk away at the left edge of a field.

3. Reaching a **barn** go left and then swing right at the next corner eventually leaving the field over a stile at a **junction of tracks**. Follow the **tarmac track** to the right. Keep going through consecutive gates, shortly winding out to a lane.

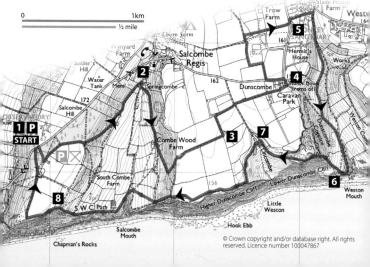

Above Salcombe Mouth on the South West Coast Path

4. Go left past **Dunscombe Cottage** before turning off over a stile on the right along a **memorial avenue**. Approaching the end, walk through a gap on the left and follow a swathe away. Turn right at the end, and approaching the next corner, look for a stile in the left hedge. An enclosed path leads to another stile, over which, go right again. The way leads on through gates between paddocks of the **Donkey Sanctuary** to meet a lane.

5. Go left and almost immediately right beside the **Sanctuary entrance**. An enclosed path leads to the main buildings. A grass path continues beyond, dropping to meet a gravel path. Follow it down right along the base of **Weston Combe** at the edge of successive small meadows, eventually reaching a kissing gate above **Weston Mouth**.

6. Through the gate, a path drops steeply to the **beach**, but the way back climbs right towards **Salcombe Mouth**. Ignore a gate to 'Weston Plats', and carry on up into trees and through a gate.

Here, as in many other small coastal settlements, fishing and small scale farming

Red Triassic sandstone at Salcombe Mouth

often went hand in hand. Sheltered by the cliffs and southward facing, Weston Plats (plots) enjoyed a warm microclimate that encouraged early crops. The well-watered, fertile soils produced an abundance of fruits, vegetables and flowers, creating a surplus that was sold in markets as far away as London. Particularly profitable were strawberries and early Branscombe potatoes, which rivalled those from Jersey.

At a junction, swing sharp left with the **Coast Path** over **Lower Dunscombe Cliff**.

There is an impressive retrospective view past Weston Mouth, while ahead, the coast runs on past Budleigh Salterton to Start Point, almost 40 miles away.

Keep your height as the path later curves inland above **Lincombe**, but then, towards the head of the valley, watch for the **Coast Path** dropping left down steps to a gate.

7. Climbing beyond, bear left to regain the cliffs and continue over **Higher Dunscombe Cliff** to a kissing gate. Keeping with the **Coast Path**, go right and then left, dropping steeply to emerge above hillside pasture. Head down half right to find a gated bridge at the bottom.

The onward route rises to the left, passing a path signed to the beach at the foot of the combe. Further along, beyond a gate, the gradient steepens onto higher cliffs,

eventually passing a **bench**, which is well sited for the view back along the coast.

8. Carry on along the **cliff top**, passing through a **kissing gate** and shortly reaching a **topograph** that identifies the landmarks along the coast. Just beyond that, turn away from the cliffs and keep with the main path, which leads back to the **car park** to complete the walk. ♦

Multicoloured cliffs

Within this short run of cliffs are strata of startlingly different rocks. The base layers are red-coloured mud and sandstones, deposited in the low-lying salt flats of an ancient hot desert. Higher up and 100 million years younger is the Upper Greensand formation, sediments from a deep-sea environment and coloured by glauconite, a greenish-yellow mineral. The thin band of white towards the top is a fossil-rich layer of limestone topped with chalk.

Boats drawn up onto the shingle at Beer, below Beer Head

Beer Head

Spectacular views, shingle beaches and an impressive underscliff are some of the highlights on this fine walk

Distance/Time: 9.5 kilometres/ 5¾ miles. Allow 3¼ to 4 hours

Start: Cliff Top Car Park, Beer (pay and display)

Grid ref: SY 227 888

Ordnance Survey map: Explorer 115: Exmouth & Sidmouth

Refreshment: Masons Arms, Branscombe | 01297 680300 | www.masonsarms.co.uk, The Old Bakery, Branscombe | 01297 680764 | www.nationaltrust.org.uk OR The Sea Shanty, Branscombe Beach | 01297 680577 | www.theseashanty.co.uk

Walk Outline

Beginning on the edge of the downs, the walk skirts Beer to the Pecorama railway-themed gardens. An old lane carries on over the hills to Branscombe, where there is refreshment and a working forge. Reaching the church, the way continues onto wooded cliff top, and down to the beach at Branscombe Mouth. The final leg explores Hooken underscliff before a final clamber over Beer Head back to the car park.

Beer

Tucked into the corner of Seaton Bay, Beer is protected from the prevailing weather and, despite lacking a harbour, offers safe haven for boats. The place grew as a fishing village, with small craft drawn onto the shingle beach as they still are today. Lace-making too developed as an industry and, also important, was limestone, quarried from caves behind the village. The stone could be finely carved before it hardened with exposure to air, and was used in the construction of many cathedrals and important buildings. Curiously, the village doesn't have a brewery, and its name derives, not from the drink, but from the forest groves that once cloaked the valley.

Above Branscombe

Bee orchid

Lovely medieval St Winifred's Church at Branscombe

The Walk

1. Leaving the **car park**'s vehicle exit, go ahead and then left along **Southdown Road.** Dropping to a T-junction, turn left and immediately leave right on a climbing path between houses. Continue over an intervening street to the top. Head right and then swing back left along **Mare Lane.**

2. Pass **Pecorama** to its car park entrance, there branching left along a hedged track, signed to 'Branscombe'. After 1.2 kilometres you reach a crossing track.

3. Cross diagonally right to a kissing gate in the hedge, from which a trod leads away across pasture. Through another gate, swing right and then left within the field corner and carry on by the right hedge. Approaching the far side, look for a stile over which the way drops into woodland. Ignoring stiles off right, head down with the main path, crossing a stile and walking on to a junction. Turn left to emerge on a lane.

4. Go right, into **Branscombe**. Keep left at successive T-junctions to pass the **Mason's Arms** and later, the v**illage hall**. Carry on past the **Forge** and **Old Bakery** (National Trust) to **St Winifred's Church**.

5. Turn in through the **churchyard**, walking down to a stile at the bottom. Over a **footbridge**, climb away, passing into **woodland**. Carry on to meet the **South West Coast Path** running along the top of the ridge.

6. Follow it left towards **Branscombe Mouth**, passing onto the National Trust's **West Cliff**. Later losing height, keep right to a **viewpoint**, dropping beyond to emerge from the wood. Cross a pasture and continue by the right hedge to a final stile at the bottom. A drive runs on past a **beach café** and over a **bridge** by **Branscombe Mouth car park**.

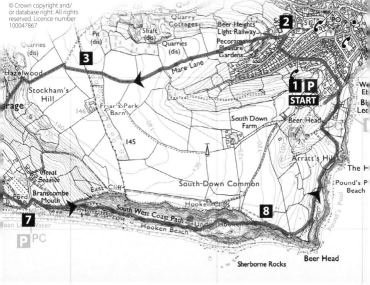

Hooken undercliff provides a priceless habitat for unusual plants and animals

7. Through a kissing gate on the right, stay with the **Coast Path** onto E**ast Cliff**. Meeting a track, follow it over a **cattle grid** into **Sea Shanty Caravan Park**. Remain on the main drive, but towards the far end, watch for the **Coast Path** branching off right. The way winds on through the thick scrub of **Hooken undercliff**.

After 800 metres, beyond a path down to the beach, the way winds up to the top of the cliffs.

The undercliff is the result of a massive overnight landslip that occurred in 1790, when some three-quarters of a mile of the 140 metre-high cliff gave way. Although fishermen out at sea reported a loud noise, the extent of the devastation was not apparent until the following morning, when it was discovered that 10 acres of coastal grazing had slumped towards the sea. Field and hedge debris were found strewn across the beach and although erosion and the incursion of scrub has since softened the scene, isolated pinnacles of towering chalk still stand from the original cliff.

The coast around Beer Head is Devon's finest location for fossil hunting, with the foreshore rather than the cliffs themselves being the best place to search. Wait for low water and look amongst the pebbles on the beach or carefully chip away at blocks,

which spring tides and stormy weather regularly dislodge from the cliff.

8. Turn right along the **cliff top**, swinging past **Beer Head** and on at the edge of the down. Eventually losing height, the way curves left down to a gate. Rise to a junction by the entrance to a **campsite** and go right to return to the **car park** to complete the walk. ♦

Fossils in the chalk cliffs

England's westernmost chalk outcrop, Hooken cliffs were deposited some 90 million years ago, an accumulation of the shells and skeletal remains of creatures inhabiting a warm prehistoric sea. Abundant are bivalves, sponges and crinoids or water lilies, but an occasional and surprising find given their fragility, are fossilised sea urchins. They belong to the same group as crinoids and starfish, all of which display a rare five-fold radial symmetry.

Useful Information

Visit South Devon
South Devon's official tourism website covers everything from accommodation and special events to attractions and adventure: **www.visitsouthdevon.co.uk**

Devon's AONBs
To learn more about South Devon's areas of oustanding natural beauty, see: **www.southdevonaonb.org.uk** or **www.eastdevonaonb.org.uk**

Jurassic Coast World Heritage Site
The Jurassic Coast website has background information on geology and fossils as well as a host of practical details to help plan your visit: **www.jurassiccoast.org**

Selected Tourist Information Centres
The main TICs provide free information on everything from accommodation and transport to what's on and walking advice.

Budleigh Salterton	01395445275
Dartmouth	01803 834224
Dawlish	01626 215665
Exeter	01392 665700
Exmouth	01395 830550
Newton Abbot	01626 215667
Salcombe	01548 843927
Seaton	01297 216600
Shaldon	01626 873723
Sidmouth	01395 516441
Teignmouth	01626 215665

Rail Travel
Main stations are located at Exeter, Newton Abbot, Totnes and Plymouth, with others serving the coast between Dartmouth and Exmouth: National Rail Enquiries 08457 484950 | **www.nationalrail.com.uk**

Bus Travel
Many places along the South Devon Coast are served by bus: **www.travelinesw.com**

Camping
Devon is a popular area for camping, with many sites owned by or affiliated to the Camping and Caravanning Club: 024 7647 5426 | **www.campingandcaravanningclub.co.uk**